Helen McGinn is a drinks expert and international wine judge, writing columns for the *Daily Mail* and *Waitrose Food* magazine. She's the author of award-winning wine blog and best-selling book *The Knackered Mother's Wine Club*. Among other awards, Helen won Online Drink Writer of the Year in Fortnum & Mason's inaugural Food & Drink Awards in 2013. She spent almost a decade sourcing wines around the world as a supermarket wine buyer and spent the next half-decade pregnant. Helen is married with three children and too many dogs. And she's hopeless with a hangover.

Twitter: @knackeredmutha
Instagram: @knackeredmother
Facebook: knackeredmotherswineclub
Website: www. knackeredmotherswineclub.com

Also by Helen McGinn
Helen McGinn's Teetotal Tipples
The Knackered Mother's Wine Club

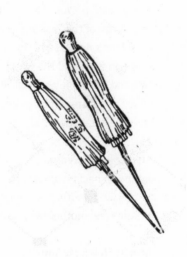

HOMEMADE COCKTAILS

HELEN McGINN

HOMEMADE
COCKTAILS

THE ESSENTIAL GUIDE TO MAKING GREAT COCKTAILS,
INFUSIONS, SYRUPS, SHRUBS AND MORE

ROBINSON

ROBINSON

First published in Great Britain in 2018 by Robinson

3 5 7 9 10 8 6 4 2

Copyright © Helen McGinn, 2018

The moral right of the author has been asserted.

A CIP catalogue record for this book is available
from the British Library.

ISBN: 978-1-47214-067-8

Designed by Andrew Barron @ Thextension
Typeset in Brandon Grotesque & Adelle
Printed and bound in Great Britain by Clays Ltd, Elcograf S.p.A.

Papers used by Robinson are from well-managed forests and other
responsible sources.

Robinson
An imprint of
Little, Brown Book Group
Carmelite House, 50 Victoria Embankment
London EC4Y 0DZ

An Hachette UK Company
www.hachette.co.uk

www.littlebrown.co.uk

'The well-made cocktail is one of the most gracious of drinks. The shared delight of those who partake ... breaks the ice of formal reserve.'

David A. Embury
The Fine Art of Mixing Drinks

CONTENTS

INTRODUCTION

COCKTAILS ARE ONE OF LIFE'S LITTLEST LUXURIES.
And suddenly they're everywhere, looking and tasting better
than ever. From swanky hotel bars to speakeasies, from classic
to themed bars, the cocktail party is in almighty full swing.
Which is fine and dandy if you're out on the town but what
about when it comes to making cocktails at home? Maybe it's
the long list of ingredients or the thought of all that mixing
and muddling, but for whatever reason we tend to reach for
a bottle of wine or beer instead. Thing is, cocktails needn't be
complicated. With just a little know-how there's a whole lot of
fun to be had with the spirit world at home.

This book is full of real drinks, simply made. The recipes will
help you make the most of the bottles you've got in your
drinks cupboard, whether you're making cocktails for one,
two or more. You'll find lots of easy homemade infusions,
syrups and shrubs along with a selection of the best classic
cocktail recipes and plenty of new ones to try. And for dry
days and non-drinkers we've got booze-free options too.

There's a list of the tools that make the mixing of drinks easier,
each with a simple alternative if you've got to improvise. Not
got a cocktail shaker? Use a jam jar. No muddler to hand? A
rolling pin will do. More on that later but for now, it's time to
break the ice.

DIFFERENT TYPES OF COCKTAIL

So what, exactly, is a cocktail? Unsurprisingly, the true origins of the cocktail are a little hazy but what we do know is that from around the eighteenth century people were drinking a combination of spirits, sugar, water and bitters and calling it a cocktail. Nowadays I think we're OK to loosen the tie on that particular description and go with anything that's a mix of two or more ingredients, at least one of which is alcoholic.

There are endless possible combinations of ingredients, just as there are with food recipes. A great cocktail is one that manages to balance the flavours and, crucially, hits the spot.

In today's crazy craft cocktail era, a lot of recipes simply riff on an old classic. We'll cover those classics in a bit – the Martini, the Negroni, the Old Fashioned, the Daiquiri and so on – but first, here's a quick explanation of some of the different types of cocktail so you can suit your drink to your mood.

SOURS

This particular family of drinks is, as the name suggests, definitely not sweet. The key ingredient is a base spirit such as gin or whisky/whiskey along with lemon or lime juice and a tiny dash of sweetness to balance the flavours. Sometimes you'll find egg whites in there too.

FIXES

These are short, uncomplicated little drinks in the sour family, a mix of your favourite spirit along with a dash of citrus juice and sugar. Usually served in a small tumbler with crushed ice.

RICKEYS

Decidedly dry with little or no sugar added is what makes a Rickey a Rickey. Usually made with gin as the base spirit and with a generous dash of something citrusy.

JULEPS

The keynote here is mint and mellow sweetness. Originally a mix of bourbon, mint, ice and sugar syrup, but you can use any spirit you like and as long as the headline act is mint supported by sweetness it's a julep.

HIGHBALLS

If you're making a highball, you'll have a tall glass with lots of ice, a measure or two of spirit and plenty of your mixer of choice. Your gin and tonic? That's a highball cocktail.

COBBLERS

A catchall name for wine-based cocktails, often made with sherry, with lots of ice and a dash of sweetness. Citrus might feature, depending on your taste/mood/what you've got in the fruit bowl.

BUCKS

This name tends to attach itself to anything with ginger beer or ginger ale in it, along with citrus – lemon, lime or orange – juice. Key requirement is a bit of a kick when it comes to flavour.

STORE CUPBOARD ESSENTIALS

As long as you've got a bottle of one of these spirits in your drinks stash, you've got the start of a great cocktail. If you have a bottle of each, you can open a bar.

Vodka

Gin

Whisky/Whiskey/Bourbon

Rum

Brandy

Tequila

If you already know (or don't need to know) the basics behind each spirit, go straight to the next bit (page 15), about other boozy ingredients. Otherwise, here's a quick what's what.

SPIRITS: THE LOWDOWN

The thing that makes spirits different from other alcoholic drinks is the art of distillation: basically, heating up a fermented liquid (made from anything from grain to potatoes to fruit), separating the water and concentrating the alcohol in what's left. And the reason this works is because alcohol boils at a lower temperature than water. So if you heat up a fermented liquid, you can collect the vapours before the water boils and cool and condense them back into a liquid. Hey presto, you've got a distilled spirit.

Distillation is done in a contraption called a pot still. It looks like an oversized copper kettle with a long neck, varying in size from one you can sit on your kitchen table to enormous great things, all producing spirits in batches.

Another type of still is a column still, sometimes known as a Coffey still. These work on a continuous process of distillation with a more predictable end result compared with a batch-producing pot still.

When the spirit first comes off the still it's completely clear but colour might come later, either if the liquid is aged in oak barrels or if something's added to give it a desired colour.

VODKA

This is your basic spirit, usually made from grain such as wheat or rye, but it can be made from anything with fermentable natural sugars, including potatoes. Because vodka is relatively neutral in flavour it makes for a cracking cocktail base and works with pretty much any other ingredient you care to throw at it. Think of it as the crisp white shirt of the spirits world. But not all vodkas are created equal. Some are more neutral in flavour, some more characterful. It really depends on where and how they're made. Traditionally vodkas from Poland, Russia and Scandinavia had a more discernible character than those from elsewhere but that's not necessarily the case now. There's plenty of choice, from delicate vodkas to more rounded, fuller-bodied ones. It's all a question of taste.

GIN

Gin basically starts life as a neutral spirit (in other words, vodka) but has added flavour from plant-based ingredients, known as botanicals. To make a good-quality gin, the neutral spirit goes into a still with the chosen flavourings and the whole lot gets redistilled. Reading like something from a wizard's recipe book, ingredients include juniper berries, coriander seeds, angelica root, orange and lemon peel and cardamom, among others. Of all the botanicals, the one that must be included in the mix for the end result to be called gin is juniper. And as juniper belongs to the conifer family, it adds that usually discernible whiff of pine, giving the drink a kind of reassuringly medicinal-in-a-good-way feel.

Most of the gin cocktails in this book are made with a type of gin (not a brand, but a legally defined type) called London Dry Gin. To know if you're buying a London Dry Gin, just look for those words on the label. It won't contain any artificial ingredients and has little or no added sugars and no flavouring or colouring after it's been distilled. And despite the name, it can be made anywhere.

WHISKIES

Made from grain and, nowadays, made all over the place. Some cocktails call for bourbon, a type of American whiskey (with an 'e') mainly from Kentucky, made from corn along with barley and rye and aged in charred oak barrels. Bourbon tends to be a little sweeter than Scotch whisky (no 'e'), which comes in two forms – malt or blended. Single malts are made from malted barley and come from a single distillery. Blended Scotch is a mix of single malt and grain (usually wheat) whiskies.

Peat bogs are a big thing in Scotch whisky production; the soil is used to fire kilns to dry the barley, infusing it with a definite smoky character. Quite how much depends on who's making it but traditionally single malts from Islay are pretty 'peaty' compared with those from everywhere else. Overall Scotch whiskies vary depending on where and how they're produced and how long they are aged in barrels; they range from light and floral to rich and smoky, with dried fruits, nuts, spice, malt and honey flavours in there too.

Irish whiskey (with an 'e') doesn't really do peat so is distinctly lighter in style compared with Scotch whisky but there are so many different styles it's hard to generalise.

There are whiskies from Canada, usually made with rye, barley or corn and known for their lighter, smoother flavours compared with Scotch and bourbon. Then there are whiskies from Japan, India and Sweden, all of which produce single malt styles.

RUM

There's no doubt about it: rum puts me in a holiday mood with its sun, sea and sandy Caribbean beach vibe. It's a spirit made from sugar cane juice or from molasses, the gloopy syrup produced by sugar during the refining process. How it's distilled, aged and blended determines the style, ranging from white to dark. White rums are made with little or no ageing and tend to be light and fresh in style compared with the coffee and chocolate flavour hit of aged-in-oak dark rum. Golden rum sits somewhere between the two in style, having spent a bit of time ageing in casks to get its colour. Then there's spiced rum, a relatively new guest at the party, typically made with flavours like cinnamon and vanilla. All in all, rum makes for a brilliant cocktail ingredient thanks to its warm, friendly flavours.

BRANDY

A spirit produced from wine made from grapes is usually called brandy. Cognac and Armagnac are two of the most famous regions for brandy, both in France. Cognac is a stone's throw from Bordeaux and the wine is distilled twice before being aged in oak barrels. Armagnac is a little further south and the wine is usually distilled only once, producing a generally fuller-bodied, fruitier style. Their mellow, dried-fruit-and-nuts flavours are a joy on their own but putting them in a cocktail means we don't have to wait until after dinner to enjoy them. Jackpot.

TEQUILA

When you're drinking tequila, you're drinking a spirit made from blue Weber agave, a plant grown in Mexico. To make it the plant is harvested, cooked, fermented and distilled. The most common type is a clear, un-aged style called *blanca*, also known as 'silver' or *plata*. *Reposado* on the label tells you that it's been aged in oak barrels for anything between a couple of months and a year; *añejo* means between one and three years; *extra añejo* for at least three years. These tend to be richer in style with weightier flavours than the un-aged tequilas.

Mezcal is also made from the agave plant but from a variety of species, while tequila comes from just one. The obvious difference between the two drinks is the pungent, smoky character that mezcal has, given by the smoking of the agave hearts, called *piñas*, when it's being made. Oh, and the worm. You won't find worms in bottles of tequila, only in some bottles of mezcal.

OTHER BOOZY INGREDIENTS

Have at least one of these in your drinks cupboard and you can make an awful lot more cocktails.

Orange fruit liqueur (triple sec)
Bitters
Campari
Vermouth
Sherry
White port
Absinthe

ORANGE FRUIT LIQUEUR

This is a spirit that's been flavoured with oranges and sweetened. Often referred to as curaçao or triple sec, so-called because it is triple distilled before being flavoured with dried (or *sec*) fruits – in this case dried orange peel. Cointreau and Grand Marnier (a Cognac-based orange fruit liqueur) are both cocktail staples and a bottle of this stuff goes a long way.

Of course there are lots of other liqueurs to choose from – other fruit ones, herby ones, coffee ones, chocolate ones (clear crème de cacao is a cocktail classic), cream ones – but orange is one of the most versatile of the lot when it comes to making cocktails.

BITTERS

When it comes to cocktails, bitters act as seasoning. Basically, it's alcohol flavoured with plant extracts to give it bitter or bittersweet flavours. I always keep a small bottle of Angostura bitters in the cupboard, occasionally alongside a bottle of orange bitters from the same makers, but there are lots more craft concoctions available now. Of course you could make your own but I feel the same about that as I do about stuffing a mushroom.

Italian *amari* (literally translated as 'bitter') are a family of after-dinner, herbal liqueurs usually sipped alongside a strong shot of espresso. They make great cocktail ingredients too, adding instant oomph.

CAMPARI

Officially a 'bitters', but however you categorise this strange beast, it's one of the hardest working ingredients in the cocktail store. Made from alcohol, water and a mix of plants, fruits and herbs, it's an orangey, herbal mash-up and essential for making a decent Negroni.

Aperol is lighter in both alcohol and flavour than the rather more serious Campari but is seriously good in a glass with prosecco and topped up with soda.

VERMOUTH

We're talking aromatised, fortified wine: in other words, wine
that's been beefed up with added spirit to make it a bit stronger
and then infused with botanicals to make it smell and taste
a certain way. Promise you it tastes better than it sounds,
especially once it's in a cocktail. For homemade cocktails
we need a sweet red one and a dry white one.

SHERRY

You know that bottle of sweet sherry you've got sitting in the
cupboard, the one you used to make trifle last Christmas? Well,
we're not wasting the rest of it. Instead, we're going to use it in a
cocktail. And the great dry sherries like fino and manzanilla are
brilliant ingredients.

PORT

I'm not talking about the red stuff – save that for the end of dinner and a hunk of cheese – but when it comes to cocktails white port is a gem. And like sherry, usually really good value for money, helped by the fact that it is (un)fairly unfashionable. Add white port to tonic and plenty of ice, garnished with plenty of fresh mint and lemon. Properly, refreshingly different.

ABSINTHE

A heady, bitter spirit flavoured with botanicals including anise and fennel, this was the drink of choice of Paris' great artists and writers back in the Belle Epoque. Well, it was before it was banned thanks to its reputation for being hallucinogenic. But now the Green Fairy (as it was known then) is back and not at all mind-bending – unless you simply drink too much of it, of course.

NON-BOOZY INGREDIENTS

BAGS OF ICE OR
TRAYS OF FRESH ICE CUBES

You'll need ice. Lots and lots of ice. I buy the big 2kg bags from the supermarket – so much easier than filling ice-cube trays that always seem to spill in the freezer tray, catching rogue frozen peas in the process. Nowadays you can get anything from normal cubes to giant cubes to crushed ice but normal cubes are the most versatile.

SUGAR SYRUP

Lots of classic cocktail recipes call for a dash of sugar syrup to balance the flavours in the glass. You can use either shop-bought or homemade syrup. It's simple enough to make: put equal amounts of sugar and warm water together in a jar and shake until combined. Or you can heat them up gently in a pan for about 5 minutes until the sugar has dissolved. It'll keep in the fridge for at least a few weeks, usually longer.

There are also lots of ready-made flavoured syrups such as orgeat (made using almonds) and falurnum (a citrus and spice mix often used in tropical fruit-based cocktails). And it's easy to make flavoured syrups using ingredients such as vanilla pods and tea. See page 61 for some recipe ideas.

MIXERS

I prefer buying mixers in single-serve cans or bottles unless I know I'm catering for a crowd. Nothing kills a cocktail like a flat mixer.

Soda water
Tonic water
Ginger ale
Ginger beer
Tomato juice

VERJUS

I can't pretend this is easy to get hold of, but when you do, you'll be very happy you did. Literally translated as 'green juice', it's a non-alcoholic juice made from unripened grapes. In the old days, it was a way of using the not-quite-good-enough grapes that were taken off the vines before harvest. In cocktails and cooking, it adds a citrusy, sour kick. If life doesn't give you fresh lemons, you can use this instead.

GARNISHES

A twist of something fresh will give the aromas and flavours of your cocktail a real boost, but we'll be making use of some things from the store cupboard and freezer too. Here are some of the most commonly used.

✳ Citrus fruits – lemons, limes, oranges
✳ Fresh seasonal berries (or a bag of frozen berries: the ones you can buy as smoothie mixes are good as they've got a mix of blueberries, redcurrants and strawberries)
✳ Fresh herbs – especially mint, rosemary and thyme
✳ Dried spices such as peppercorns (black, pink, whatever colour you've got), chilli flakes and star anise

LIQUIDS

Metric	Imperial	US cup
5ml	1 tsp	1 tsp
10ml	2 tsp	2 tsp
15ml	1 tbsp	1 tbsp
50ml	2fl oz	3 tbsp
60ml	2½fl oz	¼ cup
75ml	3fl oz	⅓ cup
100ml	4fl oz	scant ½ cup
150ml	5fl oz	⅔ cup
200ml	7fl oz	scant 1 cup
250ml	9fl oz	1 cup
300ml	½ pint	1¼ cups
350ml	12fl oz	1⅓ cups
400ml	¾ pint	1¾ cups
500ml	17fl oz	2 cups
600ml	1 pt	2½ cups
1 ltr	34fl oz	4 cups

WEIGHT

Metric	Imperial
25g	1oz
50g	2oz
100g	4oz
200g	7oz
250g	9oz
300g	10oz

EQUIPMENT, METHODS AND MEASUREMENTS

The cocktail boom has led to something of a barware bonanza, with designer drinks trollies and fancy glassware. But really, as long as you've got a clean glass of roughly the right size, you're good to go. Here's what you need, along with an alternative if you don't have the conventional barware to hand.

GLASSES

My own cocktail glass collection has grown over the last few years due to an inability to walk past a secondhand shop without scouring the shelves for old glasses. The glasses I use all hold 200ml comfortably.

Martini glass
Small tumbler (also known as a rocks glass)
Tall tumbler (also known as a highball)
Wine glass
Flute or coupe

OTHER EQUIPMENT

Jigger (or an **egg cup**) to measure your spirits. A standard shot is 25ml or just under 1 fluid ounce.

Cocktail shaker (or a **large jam jar**). My old metal shaker has lasted for years and has a built-in sieve at the top so you don't usually need to use a separate strainer.

Muddler (or a **rolling pin**): to muddle your ingredients means to gently mash them up a bit. A long-handled cocktail muddler is one way to do it, or you can use the end of a rolling pin or a mortar.

Strainer (or a **sieve**) to get any ice or other bits out as you pour the contents of the shaker into your glass. You can invest in a made-for-cocktails Hawthorne strainer or just make do with a tea strainer.

Pitcher (or any **jug**) for making cocktails for a crowd.

Stirring rod (or a **chopstick/fondue stick**) for when you need to stir rather than shake your cocktails.

Juice squeezer – you can do this by hand but a handheld metal implement sometimes called a Mexican Elbow is a game-changer.

Sharp knife and **chopping board** for cutting citrus fruits.

Peeler for removing strips of citrus fruit skin to twist and pop into your glass as a garnish.

Wooden rolling pin, clean linen towel or **freezer bags** – for crushing ice.

Kilner jars for making your own infusions.

METHODS

Some cocktails are shaken, some are stirred. Each recipe will tell you whether you're shaking, stirring or just putting everything straight into the glass.

Some recipes call for a chilled glass: five minutes in the freezer will do the trick.

The little strip of lemon, lime or orange peel you see in some cocktails is more than just a pretty garnish: freshly peeled and twisted over the glass, it releases a fine spray of citrus oils to add flavour to the drink.

MEASUREMENTS

The recipes in this book are shown in metric measurements. A single measure is 1 shot, 25ml or 1 oz. Often, a recipe calls for 15ml of citrus juice which is about a tablespoon's worth.

FIVE RULES FOR MAKING A GREAT COCKTAIL

1 Use plenty of ice
Lots of ice = stronger for longer. It'll keep the drink cold and won't dilute it so quickly. Allow for a generous handful of ice per drink: 4–6 cubes depending on the size of the glass.

2 Use good ingredients
Ingredients should be fresh and seasonal where possible. This is no time for using up the old half lemon lying at the bottom of the fridge drawer. Silk purse, sow's ear and all that.

3 Shake it like a Polaroid picture
If you're making a drink that needs shaking, make sure you shake it enough to mix all the ingredients well *and* get it cold. Do it with meaning, for at least 15 seconds.

4 It's all about balance
With a cocktail, you're mixing ingredients. Some may be sour, some may be sweet, but the art of making a good cocktail is balancing those flavours *to suit you*.

5 Keep it simple
A great cocktail need only take minutes to prepare, leaving you more time for the best bit of all – drinking it. The simple ones are the best.

1

MAKE YOUR OWN

JUST AS YOU WANT TO HAVE A STORE CUPBOARD WITH a variety of food ingredients when it comes to cooking, so it is for cocktails. And there's a really easy way to create a selection of different flavoured spirits and syrups without breaking the bank: make your own. All of these recipes are ridiculously simple and great fun to make. They look beautiful, taste delicious and what's more, make great presents.

You'll need a largish empty jar such as a Kilner jar, although for the flavoured syrups you can use an empty glass bottle. Before you start, make sure that whatever you use is properly clean. You can do this by putting it through a quick cycle in the dishwasher or soaking it in hot soapy water before leaving it to dry in a very low oven (100°C/225°F/Gas 4). For small batches that won't be sitting in the fridge for long I simply fill the jar with boiling water and leave it for 5 minutes before turning it upside down to dry on a tea towel. Up to you how fastidious you want to be. No judgement here.

Time to get mixing.

INFUSIONS

The idea behind these recipes is to allow you to play around with your favourite flavours. Go seasonal on the ingredients whenever you can. And with all of these recipes, the aim is to get a perfect balance of flavours. The added ingredients are there to infuse rather than take over the drink. Some suit being steeped in alcohol for weeks, if not months. Others need just a day or even a matter of hours to get the best out of them. Taste as you go along. And if you'd rather leave out the sugar from any of these recipes you can always add some sugar or sugar syrup at the end if you think it needs it. Generally, quick berry fruit infusions are fine without sugar thanks to the natural fruit sugars but anything herby or citrus tends to work better with a little bit of sugar to round out the flavours. The ones that are left for longer work better with sugar given that you're making something that you might want to sip on its own at some point, like sloe gin.

On quantities, I make these up in 500ml batches so that I don't have to use a whole bottle every time. If you want to use a whole bottle, just increase the quantities of other ingredients accordingly.

ROSEMARY & LIME GIN

3 sprigs of rosemary
500ml gin
50g sugar
1 lime, sliced

Put everything into a clean jar, seal and give it a gentle shake and then leave it for 6 hours, or overnight for more pungent rosemary flavours.

Strain the liquid through a sieve into a bowl and either back into the jar or into a clean bottle. Seal and store in the fridge.

SERVE

With lots of ice and topped up with tonic water or ginger ale, garnished with a twist of lime peel.

BLOOD ORANGE GIN

1 blood orange, sliced
50g sugar
500ml gin

Put the sliced orange and sugar into a clean jar and pour the gin over the top. Seal the jar, give it a gentle shake and leave to infuse for 12 hours or overnight.

Strain the liquid through a sieve into a bowl and either back into the jar or into a clean bottle. Seal and store in the fridge.

SERVE

A brilliant Negroni ingredient, or just serve it with tonic water, lots of ice and a small wedge of blood orange.

RASPBERRY GIN

I don't use sugar in this recipe as the raspberries give it some natural fruit sweetness

200g fresh raspberries
500ml gin

Rinse the raspberries and pop them into a clean jar. Pour in the gin. Seal the jar, give it a gentle shake and leave for a week in a cool, dark place. If you remember, give it a gentle shake every day, just to mix up the ingredients.

Strain the liquid into a bowl, through a fine muslin cloth if possible, to get any bits out. Otherwise a sieve will do. Then pour back into the jar or into a clean bottle. Seal and store in the fridge.

SERVE

Glorious in a Raspberry Martini (see Martini recipe on page 69) or serve it simply with plenty of ice, top it up with tonic water and add a twist of lemon peel and/or a raspberry to garnish.

PEA & MINT GIN

50g frozen peas
Leaves from 2 sprigs of fresh mint
500ml gin

Rinse the peas under a warm tap and pop them into a clean jar.
Put in the mint leaves, pour over the gin and give the jar a swirl
before leaving for no more than 6 hours. Any more than that
and the flavours start to taste stewed. Strain the liquid through
a sieve into a bowl and either back into the jar or into a clean
bottle. Seal and store in the fridge.

SERVE

I love this with tonic water and lots of ice, garnished with a
couple of frozen peas popped in the top.

SLOE GIN

Now, for this one I go big on quantities. That's because we only get to make this once a year when the sloes are out so we need to make enough to last us for the year. Obviously you've got to forage for your sloes but if you can't find any just buy them on the internet. No one has to know. Ignore the guff about picking after the first frost. Just make sure they're nice and ripe.

450g fresh sloes
200g sugar
1 litre gin
Dash of almond essence

Put your sloes in a bag and pop them in the freezer overnight to help break down the skins. When you're ready, put them into a clean jar and pour over the sugar (you could leave out the sugar at this stage and simply add sugar syrup at the end to taste if you prefer). Add the gin along with a tiny dash of almond essence (I stole this idea from my neighbour Maggie; her sloe gin was always better than mine until I got the secret ingredient out of her). Seal the jar and give it a gentle shake before leaving in a cool, dark place for at least a couple of months – three if you can wait that long.

When it's ready, strain it through a sieve into a jug before pouring back into the jar or into a clean bottle (or smaller bottles).

SERVE

Being more like a liqueur this is gorgeous sipped on its own, preferably fireside. Or try it in a Gin Fizz by pouring a single measure into a flute glass or coupe and topping up with sparkling wine. For maximum razzle make a Sloe Gin Martini (*see* Martini recipe on page 69).

EARL GREY GIN

---

2 Earl Grey teabags
500ml gin

Put the teabags into a clean jar. Pour in the gin and leave to infuse for 1–2 hours, depending on how strong you like your tea. Strain the liquid through a sieve into a bowl and either back into the jar or into a clean bottle. Seal and store in the fridge.

SERVE

Top up with tonic water, lots of ice and a twist of lemon peel. Add a dash of sugar syrup if you take sugar in your tea.

BLACKBERRY & APPLE GIN

This one needs longer than most to get more autumnal mellow flavours along with plenty of colour.

200g blackberries
1 apple, cored and chopped (leave the skin on)
200g sugar
500ml gin

Rinse the blackberries and put them into a clean jar. Add the chopped apple and sugar and pour over the gin. Seal the jar and give it a gentle shake, then leave in a cool, dark place for at least a month – longer if you have the patience. If you remember, give it a gentle shake once a week just to make sure all the ingredients are mixed.

Strain the liquid into a bowl, through a fine muslin cloth if possible, to get any bits out. Otherwise a sieve will do. Then pour back into the jar or into a clean bottle. Seal and store in the cupboard.

SERVE

Like the sloe gin this is more of a liqueur to sip fireside or after dinner. Or for a more refreshing take, try it with tonic and plenty of ice and pop a blackberry in the top (pinch one from your bag of frozen fruits on standby for smoothies).

BATHTUB GIN

Prohibition hit the US back in the 1920s and the story goes (at least one of them does) that bootleggers used their bathtubs to knock up batches of basic gin by filling them with neutral spirits and adding fruits and botanicals to make it taste better. What characterises Bathtub Gin is its yellowish hue and bold flavours. When it comes to making your own, pretty much anything goes as long as you've got juniper in there. The recipe below uses a few things from the spice rack but you can add as many as you like, including bay leaves, fennel seeds, cumin seeds or a few sprigs of fresh herbs like coriander and marjoram if you've got them. It might seem strange to start with vodka but the idea is you get to flavour it as you wish. As long as you've got plenty of juniper in there, it can be classed as gin.

500ml vodka
1 tbsp juniper berries
4 cardamom seeds, lightly crushed
½ tsp white peppercorns
3 tsp sugar
3 strips of lemon peel

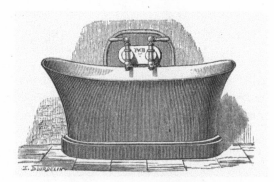

Pour the vodka into a clean jar and add all the other ingredients. Seal it and give it a gentle shake. This doesn't need long before the vodka picks up the flavours: 24 hours does the trick but leave it for 48 hours if you want it punchier still. The key is to taste as you go. Once you're happy with the balance and strength of flavour, strain the liquid through a sieve into a jug and pour back into the jar or into a clean bottle. Seal and store in the fridge.

SERVE

Go for a classic G&T with plenty of ice, topped up with good tonic and a twist of lemon peel. What's more, I suggest you drink it in the bath.

PINK PEPPERCORN VODKA

Don't be tempted to use black peppercorns: it'll leave you with vodka the colour of dishwater. And even though the main thing about infusions is flavour, I like mine to look good too!

2 tbsp pink peppercorns
500ml vodka

Put the pink peppercorns into a clean jar and pour over the vodka. Seal, give it a gentle swirl and then leave to infuse for 24 hours.

Strain the liquid through a sieve – if possible, lined with muslin cloth to get all the bits out – into a jug and pour back into the jar or into a clean bottle. Seal and store in the fridge.

SERVE

The peppery kick makes this a natural fit for a Bloody Mary (see page 79). Otherwise, simply add it to a glass with lots of ice and top it up with tonic. Add a twist of lemon and pop a couple of pink peppercorns into the glass.

RHUBARB VODKA

300g fresh rhubarb
50g sugar (optional)
500ml vodka

Rinse the rhubarb and roughly chop into cubes before putting them into a clean jar. Add the sugar if using and pour over the vodka. Seal it and give it a gentle shake. Leave it to infuse overnight or for up to 24 hours. Strain the liquid through a sieve into a jug and pour back into the jar or into a clean bottle. Seal and store in the fridge.

Boil down the leftover rhubarb with a bit of water and sugar and you've got a cheeky compote, perfect for dolloping on ice cream or on your granola in the morning.

SERVE
This is a dream with ginger ale. Just fill a highball with ice, add a measure of rhubarb vodka and top up with ginger ale and a twist of lemon peel.

TURKISH DELIGHT VODKA

Use whatever Turkish delight you prefer (my favourite's a mix of rose and lemon, but if you love the taste of rose, go full rose).

200g Turkish delight
500ml vodka

Rinse the Turkish delight under the tap to wash the sugar off (otherwise the liquid goes very cloudy) and pop it into a clean jar. Pour over the vodka, put the lid on and give it a gentle shake. Leave it for at least a week (this one does need a bit of time to get that delightful flavour infused).

When it's got the right amount of Turkish delight taste for you, strain the liquid into a jug before pouring back into the jar or into a clean bottle. Seal and store in the fridge.

SERVE
Given the fairly delicate flavour of this one, keep it simple. Add it to a glass with crushed ice and top up with soda water and a twist of lemon peel. Or make a killer Martini garnished with a sprinkling of dried rose petals and a twist of lemon peel (see Martini recipe on page 69).

WATERMELON VODKA

Half a small watermelon, cubed and skin cut off
500ml vodka

Put the cubed watermelon into a clean jar and pour over the vodka. Seal and give it a swirl. Leave it for couple of days before straining it into a jug and then pouring back into the jar or into a clean bottle. Seal and store in the fridge.

SERVE

Makes a gorgeous summer drink with tonic or soda water, plenty of ice and a twist of lemon peel.

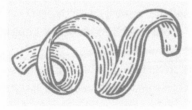

LIMONCELLO

No, come back. This is nothing like the stuff that hits you on the back of the head at the end of dinner, sledgehammer style. Honestly, this is limoncello 2.0. The recipe is so simple and the result is fresh and sweet and moreish. Just as good limoncello should be.

3 ripe unwaxed lemons
500ml vodka
300g sugar
300ml boiling water

Grate the peel of all three lemons into a clean jar and pour over the vodka. Seal and give it a gentle shake before leaving it for a week in a cool, dark place. Shake it every day if you remember. After a week, it's time to add the sugar. Put the sugar in a bowl or pan and add the boiling water, stirring until it has dissolved. Leave to cool. Add this to the jar with the vodka and lemon peel and leave it for another week. Again, give it a quick shake every day if you can.

When ready, strain the liquid into a jug and pour it back into the jar or into a clean bottle. Seal and store in the fridge.

SERVE

Serve it with lots of ice and topped up with lemonade, garnished with a twist of lemon peel. Or use it in a Lemon Martini (see page 69). Of course you can always serve straight from the freezer in shot glasses at the end of dinner.

Go crazy and make ice cream with it: make a syrup by heating the juice of 4 lemons along with 200g of caster sugar, leave it to cool; whip 500ml of double cream to soft peaks; add the syrup to the whipped cream with 4 tablespoons of limoncello; pour it into a container and put it in the freezer, giving it a stir every half an hour or so until it's more or less frozen.

CHOCOLATE VODKA

500ml vodka
50g cocoa nibs

Put the vodka into a clean jar and add the cocoa nibs. Seal and give it a gentle shake, then leave for at least 12 hours or overnight before tasting. You might find that it's chocolate-y enough for you but if not, leave it until the next day and taste again. I love dark chocolate, so for me, around three days is perfect to get that real cocoa hit and a wonderful dark colour. When you're ready, strain the vodka into a jug and pour it back into the jar or into a clean bottle. Seal and store in the fridge.

SERVE

Serve with lots of ice and top up with soda water or ginger ale and a twist of orange peel.

BLACKBERRY RUM

250g fresh blackberries
100g sugar
500ml golden rum

Rinse the blackberries and put them into a clean jar. Pour over the sugar and the rum. Seal the jar, give it a gentle shake and leave it for at least a month, two if you can. This gives it time to get that lovely colour and flavour out of the berries and infuse with the (already pretty complex) flavours of the golden rum.

Strain the liquid into a bowl, through a fine muslin cloth if possible, to get any bits out. Otherwise a sieve will do. Then pour back into the jar or into a clean bottle. Seal and store in a cool place.

SERVE

This is rather liqueur-like and lovely to sip on its own. But I love it just as much served with lots of crushed ice and topped up with soda water, finished with a twist of lemon peel.

PINEAPPLE RUM

---

1 small pineapple (about 300g), cubed
20g sugar (optional)
500ml white rum
Fresh ginger (optional)

Put the pineapple chunks into a clean jar and pour over the sugar (optional, but a touch rounds out the end flavour) and then the rum. Seal and leave overnight or for up to 24 hours. If you have it to hand, peel a thumb of fresh ginger and chuck it in with the pineapple too.

When ready, strain the liquid into a jug and pour it back into the jar or into a clean bottle. Seal and store in the fridge.

SERVE

This is one of my favourite infusions, served in a glass full of ice and topped up with ginger ale. Or try it with soda instead of ginger ale and garnish with a sprig of mint.

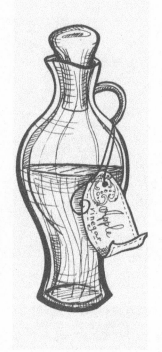

SHRUBS

First things first, we're not talking gardening. Shrubs in this context refer to non-alcoholic concoctions usually made from fruit, sugar and vinegar. Think of them as a kind of sweet and sour syrup. They're a doddle to make and can transform a drink in a flash (or rather, a dash). I started making my own shrubs to make my non-drinking days more interesting but they're just as versatile in cocktails too. Here are a few simple shrub recipes to get you going, but you can make them with pretty much any fruit you like. Use whatever's in season where possible. For the vinegar, a lighter coloured one is preferable so that the colour of the fruit comes through. Apple cider vinegar is good but otherwise just use white malt vinegar.

HOW TO SERVE

Shrubs are a sure-fire way to make a simple glass of sparkling water more interesting. I often drink mine with lots of ice and topped up with soda water or plain tonic water. These also do the trick if you've got a cheap bottle of sweetish sparkling wine that could do with a bit of pimping, like Asti or that cut-price prosecco that turned out to be not quite as good as you'd hoped. Add a dash to a flute or coupe and top up with sparkling wine for brilliantly coloured fizz with lots of flavour.

STRAWBERRY & BASIL SHRUB

250g fresh strawberries
250ml apple cider vinegar
250g sugar
Handful of fresh basil leaves

Rinse and slice the strawberries and put them into a clean jar. Pour in the vinegar, sugar and basil leaves. Gently muddle the ingredients in the jar (if you haven't got a muddler, lightly crush them against the bottom of the jar with the end of a rolling pin or mortar) and then seal the lid and shake vigorously for about 15 seconds. Leave in a cool place overnight.

Strain the liquid into a jug and pour it back into the jar or into a clean bottle. Seal and store in the fridge and it'll keep for at least six months.

BLUEBERRY & THYME SHRUB

250g fresh blueberries
250ml vinegar
250g sugar
Few sprigs of fresh thyme

Rinse the blueberries and put them into a clean jar. Pour in the vinegar and sugar and pop in a couple of sprigs of thyme. Give it all a gentle muddle (if you don't have a muddler to hand, use the back of a spoon or the end of a rolling pin) and then seal and shake vigorously. Leave in a cool place overnight.

Strain the liquid into a jug and pour it back into the jar or into a clean bottle. Seal and store in the fridge and it'll keep for at least six months.

SPICED PEAR SHRUB

250g fresh pears (about 4–5 pears)
250g sugar
Mix of spices (6 juniper berries, 6 cloves, 1 star anise,
3 cardamom pods, 6 peppercorns, ½ tsp ground cinnamon)
250ml vinegar

Peel and dice the pears and put them into a clean jar. Put the sugar on top and pop in the spices. Pour over the vinegar. Give all the ingredients a good stir, then seal the lid and shake it like you mean it. Leave in a cool place for a week. This one needs a little longer so the flavours can mellow.

Strain the liquid into a jug and pour it back into the jar or into a clean bottle. Seal and store in the fridge and it'll keep for at least six months.

FLAVOURED SYRUPS

Of course you can save time by buying a bottle of flavoured syrup – there are lots available – but you'll save money by making your own. When making flavoured syrups use a 2:1 sugar:water ratio (rather than 1:1) for a more concentrated flavour and you won't have to use as much. They'll keep in the fridge for a couple of weeks if not longer. And remember these are to add in dashes rather than big measures to cocktails, so a little goes a long way.

Use any favourite herbs like basil or mint, spices like cloves or cinnamon or even seasonal fruits or vegetables. Just make up a simple sugar syrup and add the flavourings towards the end, leaving them to sit in the syrup as it cools. Taste as you go and once the flavours are just as you like them, strain and store the syrup.

Here are a few ideas for really versatile syrups. The quantities shown here make enough syrup to add in dashes and splashes to around 20 drinks: you can scale up or down depending on how much you want to make.

VANILLA SYRUP

250ml water
500g sugar
1 vanilla pod

Put the water and half the sugar into a pan and bring to the
boil. Turn down the heat to a gentle simmer and scrape out the
seeds of the vanilla pod into the pan. Add the rest of the sugar
and stir until it dissolves, then turn off the heat and leave it to
cool. Strain into a clean jar or bottle, seal and store in the fridge.

SERVE

This works brilliantly with rum so try it in your Daiquiri (see
page 96). Also loves anything with coffee (see page 80 and try
adding a dash of this to the shaker).

TEA SYRUP

250ml water

500g sugar

1 Earl Grey tea bag (or whichever tea you prefer)

Put the sugar into a pan and cover with the water. Give it a stir and add a tea bag. Gently heat to bring it to a simmer for around 7–10 minutes, stirring occasionally and tasting as you go. Turn off the heat and leave the syrup to cool. Strain into a clean jar or bottle, seal and store in the fridge.

SERVE

This loves gin so try adding a dash to a Tom Collins (see page 72) or to a G&T. Also great in a booze-free cocktail, the Strawberry & Thyme Spritz (see page 130).

LAVENDER SYRUP

250ml water
500g sugar
8–10 small sprigs of lavender (fresh or dried)

Put the water and half the sugar into a pan and bring to the boil. Turn down the heat to a gentle simmer and add the lavender to the pan. Add the rest of the sugar and stir until it dissolves, then turn off the heat and leave it to cool with the lavender still in the pan. Strain into a clean jar or bottle, seal and store in the fridge.

SERVE

Add a dash to a Martini (see page 69) or to a Tom Collins (see page 72) in place of normal sugar syrup for a floral take on it. Garnish with a sprig of fresh lavender. Also an essential ingredient in a booze-free Lavender Lemonade (see page 131).

SPICY TOMATO MIX

As lovely as some pre-bottled juices are, making your own means you can adjust the spice accordingly. And you can't beat it for freshness. It does require quite a lot of tomatoes and you will need to skin and seed them. But after that bit of faff, the rest is a doddle. This is adapted from Victoria Moore's recipe in her brilliant book, *How to Drink*. It's very different to drinking bottled tomato juice, not least because the tomatoes are fresh rather than cooked. But the flavour is amazing.

4–6 medium tomatoes
3 shakes of Tabasco sauce
Dash of Worcestershire sauce
1 squeeze of fresh lemon
Pinch of salt

Put the tomatoes in a bowl, pour boiling water over them and leave for a minute before skinning and coring them, removing the seeds. Put the tomatoes into a blender and add the rest of the ingredients before whizzing it all up. Taste and if it's not spicy enough for you chuck in half a small, deseeded fresh red chilli and whizz up again. If the juice is too thick, just loosen it with a splash of water.

Store in the fridge but drink it on the day it's made.

SERVE
Makes enough for a decent Bloody Mary (see page 79).

2

SIMPLE COCKTAIL RECIPES

OVER THE YEARS I'VE JOTTED DOWN THE RECIPES that work for me in a little (hot pink) notebook. And this, here, is a list of favourites.

Making any drink really is a question of taste – specifically, your taste. And as with a food recipe, you can always dial up (or down) any ingredient so that the end result works for you. Use these recipes as a guideline, then tinker as you please. Make them with your own homemade infusions. Go crazy with your garnishes. Or just keep it really simple and stick to the basic recipe. However you choose to mix it up, you'll end up with a great cocktail.

GIN COCKTAILS

CLASSIC MARTINI

———

To make a Martini, you only need two liquid ingredients: gin and vermouth. But how much of each you like is a question of taste (and what sort of day you've had). How 'wet' or 'dry' you like your Martini depends on how much vermouth you like – the less vermouth, the drier the drink – and then there's the question of whether you like it shaken, stirred or dirty (in other words, served with an olive and/or olive brine in it). Here's how I like mine.

50ml gin
15ml dry vermouth
Twist of lemon peel

Before you reach for the gin, put the glasse(s) in the freezer while you put the drink together. Chuck a handful of ice into a cocktail shaker and pour in the gin, add the vermouth and give it all a good stir for about 30 seconds. Strain it into the chilled glass and twist a strip of lemon peel over the glass to release the oils before dropping it into the glass. Serve straight away. And remember what Dorothy Parker said. Two at the very most.

Don't forget to try this out with your infused gins. I love it made with Raspberry Gin (*see* page 36), topped off with a frozen raspberry pinched from the frozen smoothie mix in the freezer.

THE BRAMBLE

1984 was a good year. Not only did it give us 'Wake Me Up Before You Go-Go' by Wham!, it gave us the Bramble cocktail. Dick Bradsell, one of the biggest names in London bartending (he also created the Espresso Martini – *see* page 80. Enough said), created this blackberry-kissed gin cocktail that year and a modern classic was born. The original recipe calls for crème de mûre, a liqueur made from blackberries, but I use a cassis liqueur because I've always got some in my store cupboard (essential for Kir Royale). If you don't have either of those to hand, use sloe gin instead.

50ml gin
20ml fresh lemon juice
15ml sugar syrup
20ml crème de mûre (or crème de cassis or sloe gin)

Put a handful of ice into a cocktail shaker and add the gin, lemon juice and sugar syrup. Shake well and strain into a tumbler filled with crushed ice. Pour the crème de mûre (or crème de cassis or sloe gin) over the top and watch it turn the whole thing a really pretty colour. If you've got one, pop a blackberry into the glass.

Substitute a homemade lavender syrup (see page 64) for the sugar syrup for a more floral take on this.

NEGRONI

This is Italy's teatime drink. At least that's how I like to think of it, but whatever, this is one of the most perfect pre-dinner drinks if you want to wake up the taste buds and get the juices flowing ready for food. This recipe calls for a mix of equal parts gin, Campari and red vermouth. Make sure it's served really cold. And in small glasses – it's deceptively strong.

40ml gin
40ml Campari
40ml sweet red vermouth
Twist of orange peel or slice of orange

Fill a small tumbler with ice and then pour in each of the ingredients before giving a quick few stirs and adding a twist of orange peel or a slice of orange.

If you want to make it sloe, swap the gin for sloe gin for a rather more winter-friendly cocktail.

TOM COLLINS

A classic cocktail calling for gin, lemon juice, sugar syrup, soda and ice. Served in a tall glass, this is one of my favourite long drinks and – thanks to its simplicity – is easy to pimp with seasonal ingredients. Here's the basic recipe.

50ml gin
20ml fresh lemon juice
15ml sugar syrup
Soda water

Fill a tall glass with ice and add all the ingredients. Give it a stir, top up with cold soda water and add a twist of citrus peel – lemon, orange, lime, whatever you fancy. In summer, add fresh raspberries. In autumn, add a couple of fresh blackberries.

GIMLET

The divine mix of gin and lime was said to be drunk aboard
English naval ships to help prevent scurvy, but whatever the
medicinal properties, these two ingredients will definitely make
you feel better. The original recipe calls for lime cordial but if
you don't have any to hand, use fresh limes and a dash of sugar
syrup instead.

50ml gin
15ml lime cordial or 15ml fresh lime juice
Dash of sugar syrup (if using fresh lime juice)
Twist of lime peel

Put a handful of ice into a cocktail shaker and pour in the gin
and lime cordial, or fresh lime juice and a dash of sugar syrup.
Shake and strain into a small coupe and garnish with a twist
of lime peel, twisting it over the glass to release the oils into
the drink.

GIN & JAM

I found this recipe in the beautiful book *Regarding Cocktails* by the late Sasha Petraske, owner of New York speakeasy Milk & Honey. He called it the Cosmonaut and it's one of the simplest cocktails to make; the colour is fabulous and it balances sweet and sour flavours brilliantly. I've adjusted the original recipe a touch to suit my (rather tart) taste.

50ml gin
20ml fresh lemon juice
1 heaped tsp raspberry jam

Put a handful of ice into a cocktail shaker and pour in the gin and the lemon juice. Add the jam and shake it with meaning. Strain it into your (chilled if possible) coupe and serve. No garnish required. Told you it was simple.

G&T

I'm not going to tell you how to make a G&T other than remind you that you need lots of ice, properly cold ingredients and something fresh to garnish it. But as much as I love a twist of lemon or lime, there are lots of other really simple options when it comes to complementing the headline flavour in your chosen gin (and tonic). Play around with pairings like basil and strawberry or lemongrass and coriander seeds, or try adding a touch of honey or a pinch of salt flakes. Here are some of my favourites:

JUNIPER-RICH GINS

Juniper berries
Chilli flakes
Fresh sage leaf

CITRUS GINS

Frozen blueberries
Sprig of rosemary
Sprig of lemon thyme

FLORAL GINS

Wedge of lime
Dried rose petals
Sprig of lavender

SLOE GINS

Wedge of pink grapefruit
Star anise
Cinnamon stick

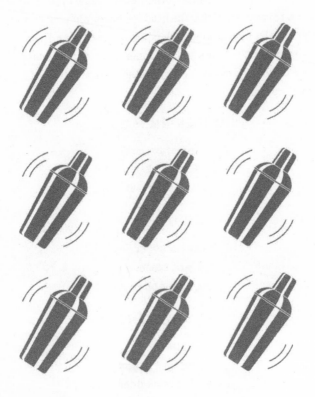

VODKA COCKTAILS

VODKA MARTINI

———

For purists a Martini should only ever be made with gin and vermouth. But there's so much fun to be had with vodka and vermouth, I'm fine with impure. Just swap the gin for your vodka of choice and off you go. Of course you could stick to normal vodka but this is where the homemade infusions make things really interesting. Try the recipe below but with Turkish Delight Vodka (see page 46), garnished with a few rose petals and a twist of lime.

50ml vodka
15ml dry vermouth
Twist of lemon peel

Put a handful of ice in a cocktail shaker and pour in the vodka, add the vermouth and give it all a good stir (or shake, if you prefer) for about 30 seconds. Strain it into the glass and add your garnish depending on the vodka you've used.

LEMON MARTINI

For this one, use your homemade Limoncello (see page 48) in place of vermouth and you've got a lip-smacking fresh new take on a Martini.

50ml vodka
25ml limoncello
15ml fresh lime juice
Twist of lemon peel

Put your coupe or martini glass in the freezer for a few minutes. Put a handful of ice in a cocktail shaker and pour in the vodka, limoncello and lime juice. Give it a good stir (or shake, if you prefer) and strain into the chilled glass. Garnish with a twist of lemon peel.

BLOODY MARY

Now, some recipes for this classic are long. I favour a simple approach but the one ingredient that I think makes the most brilliant difference is fino sherry. It really is the ultimate zhuzh-er for a bloody Mary.

50ml vodka
150ml tomato juice
Black pepper
Celery salt (or normal salt)
Worcestershire sauce
Tabasco sauce
Fino sherry
Fresh lemon
Celery stick

Put a handful of ice in a tall glass or tumbler and pour in the vodka. Top up with tomato juice (you can of course use your homemade juice, *see* page 65. Otherwise a good-quality shop-bought one will do). Add a twist of black pepper, a pinch of celery salt, a dash of Worcestershire sauce, a few drops of Tabasco and a generous dash of fino sherry. Add a squeeze of fresh lemon and stir with a celery stick. Leave the celery in as a garnish.

ESPRESSO MARTINI

Allegedly invented by Dick Bradsell for a supermodel who walked into a Soho bar and asked for something that would both wake her up and f*ck her up. Now, I'm not sure she specified that it had to be absolutely delicious to boot but luckily for the rest of us, it really, really is.

40ml vodka
20ml coffee liqueur
40ml fresh espresso coffee

Before you start, put your martini glass in the freezer. Put a handful of ice in a cocktail shaker and pour in the vodka. Then pour in the coffee liqueur (I use a cold brew coffee liqueur – so, so smooth) and lastly a freshly made espresso coffee. I know it's hot but give it 30 seconds in a cocktail shaker with lots of ice and trust me it'll be cold. Strain it into the cold glass and serve. Garnish with a couple of coffee beans if you have some. If this doesn't wake you up, I don't know what will.

SILVER BULLET

This made the list when friends asked for a cocktail including kümmel, the caraway-flavoured liqueur that so many of us have lurking in the back of the cupboard. Until then, the only way I'd drunk kümmel was very chilled, very late at night or halfway up a big hill trying to keep warm on a bracing long walk. Here's how to drink it in decidedly more glamorous fashion, with vodka as a supporting act to kümmel's reassuringly medicinal flavours. The original Silver Bullet cocktail recipe calls for gin and lemon juice, but this is a refreshing (and not quite so lethal) take on it.

25ml vodka
25ml kümmel
15ml fresh lime juice
Twist of lime peel

Crush a handful of ice in a cloth or bag, using a rolling pin, and put it into a flute glass. Put a handful of ice in a cocktail shaker and pour in the vodka, then the kümmel and finally the lime juice. Shake it and strain into the glass over the crushed ice. Garnish with a twist of lime peel.

VODKA &...

As with the G&T, I'm not going to tell you how to make a vodka and tonic/soda/whatever apart from reminding you of the need for lots of ice, properly cold ingredients and something lovely to garnish it. But now that you've got some beautiful homemade vodka infusions to play with, your vodka and tonic/soda/whatever just got more fun. Here are a few ideas.

RHUBARB VODKA & SODA

50ml Rhubarb Vodka (see page 45)
20ml fresh lemon juice
Dash of sugar syrup
Soda water
Twist of lemon peel

Put a handful of ice into a tall glass or tumbler. Add the vodka, lemon juice and sugar syrup and stir before topping up with straight-from-the-fridge soda water. Garnish with a twist of lemon peel.

DELIGHTFUL VODKA FIZZ

25ml Turkish Delight Vodka (see page 46)
Prosecco
Dried rose petals and a twist of lemon peel to garnish

Pour the vodka into a chilled coupe and top up with prosecco. Garnish with a couple of dried rose petals and a twist of lemon peel.

V&TEA

A vodka, lime and soda is so simple, so refreshing, but if
you want to shake it up a bit, add a dash of your homemade
Earl Grey tea syrup.

50ml vodka
15ml fresh lime juice
10ml tea syrup (see page 63)
Soda water
Wedge of lime

Put a handful of ice in a cocktail shaker and add the vodka, lime
juice and tea syrup. Give it all a shake and then strain into a
tumbler filled with ice. Top up with soda to taste and add a
wedge of lime, giving it a gentle squeeze over the glass as you
pop it in.

TEQUILA COCKTAILS

I haven't slammed tequila since my twenties. OK, maybe once, but the recovery time is far too long at my age. These days if I'm drinking tequila I'm sipping it neat if it's a really good one. Otherwise I'm drinking it in a cocktail. I say tequila but you can use its smokier cousin mezcal if that's what you've got to hand.

MARGARITA

The most famous tequila cocktail of them all is, honestly, one of the simplest to make. This is what you call a party starter.

Wedges of lime
Crushed sea salt (optional)
50ml tequila
20ml triple sec (see page 16)
20ml fresh lime juice

Put a coupe or small tumbler in the freezer for a couple of minutes. If you want, salt the rim of your glass by running a wedge of lime around the top and then dipping it into a bowl of crushed sea salt. Put a handful of ice in a cocktail shaker and pour in the tequila, triple sec and lime juice. Shake and strain into the chilled (and salted) glass. Add a fat wedge of lime to garnish.

DIABLO

Named after the devil, this is in fact devilishly good, with brilliant colour and flavour thanks to the addition of crème de cassis.

50ml tequila
20ml crème de cassis
30ml fresh lime juice
Ginger beer
Wedge of lime

Put a handful of ice in a cocktail shaker and add the tequila, crème de cassis and lime juice. Shake and strain into a tall glass or tumbler filled with ice. Top up with cold ginger beer and garnish with a wedge of lime.

PALOMA

This puts tequila and grapefruit together in a glass – what a good idea – and you're far more likely to come across this in bars in Mexico than you are a Margarita. I love it with pink grapefruit juice, for the colour as much as the taste.

50ml tequila
30ml pink grapefruit juice
15ml fresh lime juice
10ml sugar syrup
Soda water
Wedge of pink grapefruit or lime to garnish

Fill a tall glass or tumbler with ice and pour in the tequila, pink grapefruit and fresh lime juice. Add the sugar syrup and stir before topping up with soda water. Garnish with a wedge of lime or pink grapefruit.

WHISKY COCKTAILS

I also mean whiskey. (If this doesn't make sense, it's because you skipped the theory part. Go back to page 11 for an explanation. I won't tell anyone.) Anyway, we now get to the part about cocktails made with the whiskies of the world. You'll know what to use from your store cupboard from the spelling.

OLD FASHIONED

One of the things on my bucket list was drinking a Manhattan (bitters, sweet vermouth and whiskey) in Manhattan. I got to do just that a few years ago but soon realised that actually I prefer another classic American cocktail, the Old Fashioned. Not for the fainthearted, this one. Traditionally this drink has maraschino cherries but given that I don't often have them in the cupboard I sometimes make this without the cherry on the top and it's still delicious.

2 slices of orange
2 maraschino cherries (optional)
10ml sugar syrup
Dash of bitters
50ml bourbon

Get a tumbler and add a slice of orange cut in half, one of the cherries (if using) and the sugar syrup and bitters. Muddle the orange (and cherry) in the glass and then take out the peel/skin, leaving a puddle of fruit juice, bitters and sugar syrup at the bottom of the glass. Add a handful of ice before adding the bourbon and giving it a gentle stir. Add more bitters or sugar syrup to taste and top with a half slice of orange and a cherry (if using).

To make a Sazerac, New Orleans' most famous cocktail, follow the Old Fashioned formula but rinse the glass with absinthe first. Don't bother with the orange and cherry, just add a strip of lemon peel at the end, twisting it over the glass to release the oils into the drink. Authenticity calls for rye whiskey and Peychaud's bitters but use whatever whiskey and bitters you've got to hand and you'll still end up with a gem of a cocktail.

MINT JULEP

The official drink of America's famous horse race, the Kentucky Derby, this brings mint, sugar and bourbon together in a glass along with plenty of crushed ice. It's sweet and minty as you'd expect and, as much as I love it, I add a dash of bitters to mine.

5 fresh mint leaves, plus a couple to garnish
15ml sugar syrup
50ml bourbon
Dash of bitters (optional)

Put the mint leaves and sugar syrup in a tumbler and muddle. Add the bourbon and top up with plenty of crushed ice, as much as the tumbler will hold. Give it a stir, adding a dash of bitters if using (taste it first) and garnish with fresh mint leaves. Sip slowly so you get to enjoy the progressively mellower flavours as the ice melts.

BOULEVARDIER

Swap the gin in a Negroni for bourbon or rye whiskey and you've got yourself a Boulevardier, a cocktail created in the 1920s for an American-born, Paris-dwelling editor of a magazine of the same name called Erskine Gwynne. Remember to toast him when you make one. Also delicious made with whisky.

50ml bourbon (or whisky)
40ml Campari
40ml sweet red vermouth
Slice of orange or twist of lemon peel

Put a handful of ice into a cocktail shaker and pour in the ingredients. Give everything a stir before straining into a (preferably chilled) tumbler. Garnish with a slice of orange or a twist of lemon peel.

SCOTCH COLLINS

Like the Tom Collins (see page 72) but with whisky instead of gin. Basically it's a fancy Scotch and soda using lemon juice and sugar syrup to mix it up. There's a bit more lemon juice than in the gin version because the whisky can take it.

50ml whisky
25ml fresh lemon juice
15ml sugar syrup
Soda water
Twist of lemon peel

Put a handful of ice in a tall glass or tumbler. Pour in the whisky, lemon juice and sugar syrup and give it a stir. Top up with chilled soda to taste and garnish with a twist of lemon peel, releasing some of the oils into the glass as you twist it.

RUM COCKTAILS

Guaranteed to put you in a holiday mood, whatever the weather. White rum is the hardest working style when it comes to cocktails but there's a recipe for all styles here.

MOJITO

———

Cuba's liquid calling card is a fabulous mash-up of white rum, sugar, lime, mint and soda. There's a bit of muddling involved at the beginning but other than that, it just needs a quick stir.

10–12 fresh mint leaves, plus extra to garnish
15ml sugar syrup
20ml fresh lime juice
50ml white rum
Soda water
Wedge of lime

Put the mint leaves in a tumbler along with the sugar syrup and lime juice and lightly muddle. Add the rum and half-fill the glass with crushed ice. Give it all a stir before topping up with more crushed ice and pouring in some soda to taste. Add a sprig of fresh mint and a wedge of lime, giving it a squeeze over the glass before popping it in.

DAIQUIRI

Like the Mojito, this is a Cuban classic. To mix things up a bit, you can add fruit. Or top it up with sparkling wine to make an Old Cuban.

50ml white rum
30ml fresh lime juice
20ml sugar syrup
Wedge of lime

Before you start, put your glass (or glasses) into the freezer (I use a coupe or martini glass). Then put a handful of ice into a cocktail shaker and add the rum, lime juice and sugar syrup. Give it a good shake and strain into the chilled glass. Garnish with a wedge of lime, squeezed gently over the glass before dropping it in.

To make a fruit-flavoured daiquiri, put a handful of your fruit of choice into the cocktail shaker and muddle before adding the rum, lime juice and sugar syrup. Then shake and put through a strainer into your glass. Strawberries work brilliantly; pineapple and mango too. Mix them all up together if you're feeling really fruity.

HONEY BEE

I found this recipe in *Esquire's Handbook for Hosts*, printed more than 60 years ago and given to me by my stepmother. It belonged to her father and is so stuffed with tips on food, drink and priceless parlour games that simply reading it makes me want to throw a party. Anyway, this is one of my favourite cocktails in the book, slightly tweaked so it doesn't knock you out quite like it would have done back in 1954.

50ml white rum
15ml fresh lemon juice
15ml runny honey
Twist of lemon peel

Put a handful of ice into a cocktail shaker and add the rum, lemon juice and honey. Shake well and strain into a chilled coupe. Garnish with a twist of lemon peel.

DARK 'N' STORMY

Time to go to the dark side. This one calls for dark rum to give the drink more brooding flavours; think molasses and raisins. And the stormy bit comes from the addition of ginger beer.

50ml dark rum
25ml fresh lime juice
Ginger beer
Wedge of lime

Put a handful of ice in a tall glass or tumbler. Add the rum and lime juice. Give it a stir and top up with ginger beer. Add a wedge of lime, squeezing it over the top before dropping it into the glass.

CUBA LIBRE

This is, basically, rum and coke. But what makes it so delicious is the combination of golden rum with fresh lime juice. Using a really good cola mixer makes a big difference too, supporting the rum and lime flavours rather than smothering them.

50ml golden rum

15ml fresh lime juice

Cola

Wedges of lime

Fill a tall glass or tumbler with a handful of ice, pour in the rum and lime juice and give it all a stir. Top up with cola before squeezing a wedge of lime over the top and dropping it, together with another fresh wedge, into the glass.

PINA COLADA

This is a really simple take on one of the guiltiest of cocktail pleasures. Hum *The Pina Colada Song* as you sip.

50cl golden rum
50cl coconut milk
70cl fresh pineapple juice
15ml sugar syrup
15ml fresh lime juice

Put a handful of ice cubes in a bag or wrap in a cloth and bash them with a rolling pin, then put the crushed ice into a tumbler. Add a handful of ice cubes to a cocktail shaker and add the rum, coconut milk, pineapple juice, sugar syrup and lime juice and shake. Pour into the glass over the crushed ice. Go crazy with the garnish – pineapple slice, cocktail umbrella, flamingo swizzle stick – or just stick a straw in it and get going.

BRANDY COCKTAILS

So often the drink left until after dinner, I love the fact
that putting Cognac or Armagnac into a cocktail gives us the
excuse to drink it beforehand. With its warm Christmas cake
flavours, brandy makes a great cocktail base when put with
the right ingredients.

SIDECAR

The original recipe calls for Cognac but it's just as lovely with
Armagnac. A real classic, this'll turn your kitchen into the
coolest speakeasy within minutes.

50cl brandy
20cl triple sec
20cl fresh lemon juice
Twist of orange peel

Put a handful of ice into a cocktail shaker and add the brandy,
triple sec and lemon juice. Shake it and strain into a (chilled)
coupe glass. Garnish with a twist of orange peel.

BRANDY ALEXANDER

We used to make a round of these on Christmas Day, just
when you thought you couldn't move from the sofa.
As pick-me-ups go, these are pretty impressive. Not to mention
totally luxurious.

50ml brandy
50ml crème de cacao
50ml single cream
Grated nutmeg to garnish

Put a handful of ice into a cocktail shaker and add the brandy,
crème de cacao and cream. Shake well and strain into chilled
martini glasses. Grate a bit of nutmeg or sprinkle a pinch of
ground nutmeg over the top and serve.

SPARKLING COCKTAILS

When it comes to choosing which sparkling wine to use, some cocktails suit drier styles while others benefit from something with a bit of sweetness. I'll let you know when I think it matters. Otherwise use whatever sparkling wine you have in the fridge and ready to go.

CLASSIC CHAMPAGNE COCKTAIL

This drink involves champagne, brandy and a sugar lump. See how fun – and easy – cocktails can be?

Sugar lump
Dash of bitters
20cl brandy
Champagne
Twist of orange peel

Put your flute or coupe in the freezer for a couple of minutes while you get the other ingredients together. Take your sugar lump and shake a few drops of bitters on to it. Drop it into your chilled glass and pour in the brandy. Top up with champagne and garnish with a twist of orange peel.

FRENCH 75

This is my all-time favourite champagne cocktail. But these days I make it with English sparkling wine as much as I do with champagne. This works with prosecco, cava or crémant too but here's a classic version ready for you to play with as you see fit.

25ml gin

15ml fresh lemon juice

15ml sugar syrup (less if using prosecco)

Champagne (or another sparkling wine)

Twist of lemon peel

Put a couple of ice cubes in a cocktail shaker and add the gin, lemon juice and sugar syrup. Shake and strain into a chilled flute or coupe and top up with chilled champagne. Add a twist of lemon peel.

MIMOSA

As much as I love a Bellini (puréed peach juice topped up with prosecco) I'm not so keen on making one myself. All that puréeing means that it's the kind of cocktail I like having made for me, preferably in a bar in Venice, mostly in my dreams. But this one's lovely too – and no call for purée or peaches. I tend to use cava or crémant here.

80ml chilled sparkling wine
80ml chilled fresh orange juice
10ml triple sec
Twist of orange peel

Chill your flute or coupe. Fill the glass half full with sparkling wine. Top up with fresh orange juice, and add a dash of triple sec. Garnish with a twist of orange peel.

KIR ROYALE

OK, when I said the French 75 was my all-time favourite champagne cocktail, I forgot how much I love this one too. Basically, it's all about mood. The French 75 is laser-like with its freshness. This is decidedly mellower as champagne cocktails go. And sometimes that's what's called for. And because the cassis packs lots of flavour, it can turn a mediocre sparkling wine into something far more palatable.

10ml crème de cassis
100ml chilled sparkling wine

Pour the crème de cassis into a chilled flute or coupe. Add the sparkling wine. No garnish needed – it's perfect as it is.

SHERRY COCKTAILS

A glass of chilled fino or manzanilla makes the most brilliant aperitif, so it's not surprising that sherry can work so well in a cocktail too. It's just not the first ingredient that comes to mind when making them. But try these and you'll be reaching for the sherry more often than you thought.

SHERRY COBBLER

When talking cobblers, we're talking about a (usually) wine-based cocktail with a touch of sweetness, lots of ice and some fruit. Sherry's a fortified wine so it lends itself to a cobbler quite happily.

50ml fino or manzanilla sherry
30ml fresh lemon juice
15ml sugar syrup
Slice of orange and sprig of fresh mint (optional)

Put a handful of ice into a cocktail shaker. Crush a handful of ice (put it in a bag or wrap it in a tea towel and beat it with a rolling pin) and add to a tumbler. Pour the sherry, lemon juice and sugar syrup into the shaker and shake. Strain the contents into the glass and garnish with a couple of half slices of orange and a sprig of mint if you've got some. If you want your drink a little longer, top up with soda.

ADONIS

You can make this with different types of sherry depending on what you like/what you've got in the fridge or cupboard. The original recipe calls for a measure of red vermouth but this particular recipe, given to me by top sherry mixologist Boris Iván, uses cream sherry for sweetness instead. Told you we'd find a use for trifle leftovers.

40ml dry fino sherry
30ml cream sherry
10ml oloroso sherry
Dash of orange bitters
Strip of orange peel

Put a handful of ice into a cocktail shaker and pour in all the ingredients, bar the garnish. Gently stir with a long spoon before straining into a wine glass. Add the strip of orange peel. All done.

HOT COCKTAILS

When the weather outside is frightful, it's time for something
delightful in your glass. These mellow concoctions are like
central heating for the body.

MULLED WINE

When it comes to picking a red wine to use, make sure it's fairly
robust but not too heavy and tannic. Malbec and Merlot both
work well here. This recipe calls for a bottle of wine and will
give you about eight servings.

100ml orange juice

100g muscovado sugar

Half an orange

5 cloves

Fresh ginger

Stick of cinnamon

Star anise

Vanilla pod (optional), sliced lengthways

750ml (1 bottle) red wine

50ml ruby port

Twists of orange peel

Put the orange juice and muscovado sugar in a pan and heat
gently. Add half an orange studded with the cloves, a peeled
thumb of ginger, a stick of cinnamon, a piece of star anise, the
sliced vanilla pod (if using), and the entire bottle of red wine.
Then add the port and heat gently for about 10 minutes. Serve
in glasses with a twist of orange peel and a cinnamon stick in
each if you've got them to spare.

HOT TODDY

Don't just wait until the first sign of a cold to drink this.
Prevention is better than cure and alcohol kills germs dead.
Just saying.

Fresh ginger (optional)
1 tsp runny honey
Wedge of lemon
50cl whisky or bourbon

Put a sliver of fresh ginger and a teaspoon of honey into a
heatproof glass. Pour in a little boiling water, squeeze the juice
from the lemon wedge into the glass, dropping it in afterwards.
Add the whisky or bourbon and leave to steep for 5 minutes
before drinking. Feel free to inhale while you're waiting.

MULLED CIDER

Use whatever cider you like; I love it made with a good-quality
scrumpy. This will make enough for six servings.

2 x 500ml bottles of cider
Star anise
Stick of cinnamon
6 cloves
Half an orange
30ml (2 tbsp) honey
30ml fino sherry (optional, adds an extra nip in the throat)
1 Cox's apple, sliced

Put everything except the sherry and apple into a pan and
gently heat for 10–15 minutes without letting it boil.

Add the sherry and slices of apple for the last couple of
minutes before you serve. Ladle into glasses, making sure there's
a piece of apple in each.

IRISH COFFEE

This really calls for Irish whiskey with its just-right smoothness. Lightly whipping the cream beforehand and pouring it in over the back of a spoon will ensure it floats rather than sinking to the bottom.

150ml hot black coffee (filter coffee if possible)
1–2 tsp brown sugar
50ml Irish whiskey
50ml double or whipping cream, lightly whipped
Pinch of ground nutmeg

Take a big wine glass and fill halfway with coffee, add sugar to taste and stir. Pour in the whisky and stir. Then pour a layer of cold, lightly whipped cream over the back of a teaspoon on top of the coffee. Top with a pinch of nutmeg.

BOOZY HOT CHOCOLATE

I love this with Frangelico hazelnut liqueur. If you don't have any, just use rum instead. If you're doing that, add a spoon of dulce de leche and a pinch of salt flakes for the most ridiculously delicious salted caramel version.

150ml milk
50ml double cream
15ml (1 tbsp) cocoa powder
25ml hazelnut liqueur (or rum, see above)
Sugar to taste
Whipped cream (optional)

Warm the milk in a pan then add the cream and cocoa powder. Whisk gently until well mixed. Add the hazelnut liqueur and a tablespoon or so of sugar and stir. Pour into a big mug and add the whipped cream on top if using. Now head to the sofa.

3

COCKTAILS
FOR A CROWD

THESE DRINKS CAN (MOSTLY) BE MADE AHEAD IN quantity, brilliant when having to keep a crowd happy (and lubricated). When it comes to party drinks, I prefer clean, fresh flavours to kick off a party rather than punches (orange juice only belongs in a cocktail if it's before noon in my book). Also: nothing too fiddly or fancy. I mean you want to look like you've made an effort. Just not so much of an actual one that you wish you'd just gone for wine and beer instead.

WHITE WINE CUP

Use strawberries in place of raspberries if you prefer but
I like the way raspberries hold their own in a drink like this.
Strawberries tend to go a bit mushy. This makes around
14 servings.

1.5 litres (2 bottles) dry white wine
350ml triple sec
30ml sugar syrup (optional)
1 orange, sliced
10–12 fresh raspberries
4 strips of cucumber peel
500ml soda water
Handful of edible flowers (optional)

Put everything except the soda water and flowers in a big
serving jug or punch bowl and chill for at least an hour.
When ready to serve, add plenty of ice and top up with soda
water. Add some edible flowers (if using) and serve in small
tumblers or wine glasses.

ROSÉ SUMMER COCKTAIL

Shared by a winemaking friend, Gavin Quinney, who makes a gorgeous rosé at Château Bauduc, his property in Bordeaux. Happy as I am to drink the wine on its own, this rosé summer cocktail is a great way to make it go that bit further when you've got more people to please. Makes enough for at least 25 glasses.

1.5 litres (2 bottles) rosé wine
100ml vodka
50cl cranberry juice
Juice of 1 lime
Dash of lime cordial
Ginger ale
Sprigs of fresh mint and wedges of lime to garnish

Pour the rosé, vodka, cranberry juice, lime juice and lime cordial into a jug. Chill for at least half an hour.

When ready to serve, add a handful of ice to tall glasses and pour to half full with the chilled mix. Top up with chilled ginger ale and garnish with fresh mint and a wedge of lime, giving it a squeeze before you drop it into the glass.

PISCO SOUR

I've drunk my fair share of Pisco Sours over the years thanks to
spending lots of time in South America as a wine buyer for a big
supermarket. Pisco is the spirit, made from grapes. The sour bit
comes from the addition of citrus, in this case lime juice. There's
a dash of sugar to balance the flavours and then there's egg
whites. This is the bit that had always put me off making these
in quantity – until I met Catalina. Not only is she an incredible
Chilean artist, she can whip up perfect Pisco Sours in bulk
without even breaking a sweat. Here's how. Makes enough
for 6–8 glasses. This doesn't work when made too far ahead
otherwise the drink loses its foamy lightness. Just make them
in batches as you go.

350ml pisco
100ml fresh lime juice (about 3–4 limes)
2 tbsp icing sugar
Big handful of ice cubes
1 large egg white
Strips of lime peel
Bitters (optional)

Put all the ingredients (except the lime peel and bitters) into a
blender and blend until foamy. Taste and add more icing sugar
if it needs it. Then add a few strips of lime peel and blend again.
Pour into small tumblers, flutes or coupes – and if you've got
some, add a few drops of bitters over the foam on each glass.
If you'd rather not put whole ice cubes in your blender, just
crush the ice before you put it in the blender (put it in a bag
or wrap it in a tea towel and beat it with a rolling pin).

MOSCOW MULE

The recipe is simple – vodka, ginger, lime and bubbles – but so effective. It gives a party the most brilliant kick-start and because you can mix it up ahead, you're not left shaking cocktails last minute. This makes enough for around 20 drinks.

1 litre vodka
100ml fresh lime juice (about 4 limes)
3 litres ginger beer
Fresh lime wedges to garnish

Pour the vodka and lime juice into a jug and stir. Leave in the fridge to chill for at least an hour.

When you're ready to make them, put tall glasses out along with a big bowl of ice and another filled with wedges of lime. Line up the chilled bottles of ginger beer. To serve, fill each glass with ice then pour in the vodka and lime juice mixture to a third of the way up the glass. Top up with ginger beer and add two lime wedges, squeezing one into the glass as you add it.

RASPBERRY GIN FIZZ

—

Remember that raspberry gin you made? I'm hoping you've got some left because it's the secret ingredient for one of the most delicious (and unbelievably easy) sparkling wine party cocktails. Prosecco is good here but use whatever sparkling wine you have to hand. One bottle of prosecco will give you six servings.

120ml Raspberry Gin (see page 36)
750ml (1 bottle) prosecco

Pour 20ml of raspberry gin into each chilled flute or coupe and top up with chilled prosecco. Garnish each with a fresh raspberry. If it's New Year's Eve (or you're just naff like me) add a sprinkle of edible glitter to each one.

SGROPPINO

This is more of a pudding than a cocktail but a brilliant one to make when there's a crowd around the table for dinner. Basically, it's a souped-up slushie made from lemon sorbet, vodka and prosecco (told you it was brilliant). If you've got a bottle of black Sambuca to hand, it only adds to the drama. If you don't have any black Sambuca, you could swap the vodka for your homemade Limoncello (see page 48) for an extra lemony twist. This recipe makes enough for eight servings.

8 scoops of lemon sorbet
50ml vodka
80ml prosecco
40ml black Sambuca (optional)

Put the sorbet and vodka in a blender and blitz. Gently pour on the prosecco and give it a stir to mix it all together. Divide the mixture between eight glasses and top with a teaspoon of black Sambuca in the centre of each. Serve straightaway, before it starts to separate (but I promise you, it's so delicious, it won't last that long).

COCONUT G&T

Adding coconut water to the mix gives this a completely different taste and texture, one that'll keep guests guessing until they know what it is. This makes enough for around 12 servings.

600ml gin
600ml coconut water
180ml fresh lime juice (about 6 fresh limes)
600ml tonic water
Fresh mint leaves and wedges of lime

Pour the gin, coconut water and lime juice into a jug and give it a stir, then leave in the fridge to chill until you're ready. Set out your glasses and add a handful of ice to each. Pour in the gin mixture to about halfway and top up with chilled tonic water. Add a sprig of mint and a wedge of lime to each glass, gently squeezing the lime before dropping it in.

FROZÉ (OR FRITE)

You can make this with rosé or white wine, but either way the wine needs to be frozen beforehand. And you need to make a really simple, quick raspberry syrup. But I promise the rest takes minutes to put together (and drink, it's so delicious). Serves four with a little extra left for top ups or six with no top ups.

750ml (1 bottle) rosé or white wine
60g sugar
60ml water
Handful of fresh raspberries
Juice of 1 lime
Sprigs of fresh mint and/or raspberries to garnish

The night (or early morning) before you want to drink this, pour the wine into a baking dish and put it in the freezer. It won't go completely solid thanks to the alcohol but it will go slushy. Next, you need to make raspberry syrup (you can make this ahead too). Put the sugar in a pan, add the water and heat gently until the sugar has dissolved. Scrunch the raspberries in your hands before dropping them into the pan. Turn off the heat and leave them to steep while the syrup cools. Strain into a jug. Store in the fridge if making this ahead.

When you're ready, scoop the frozen wine into a blender and add the raspberry syrup. Squeeze in the juice of the lime and top up with a handful of crushed ice. Whizz it all up and pour straight into coupes or flutes. Garnish with a sprig of mint and/or a raspberry and serve immediately.

PASSION FRUIT SHOTS

These are simple after-dinner shots, a kind of palate cleanser if you like.

70cl (1 bottle) gin
Fresh passion fruit (half per person)

All you need to do is put a bottle of gin (and shot glasses) in the freezer before your party. Then when you're ready to serve, cut a passion fruit in half and squeeze the contents of one half into a glass. Repeat depending on how many you need. Then pour in the ice-cold gin and serve. Drink it in one go.

PICKLEBACKS

If you don't like pickles, look away now. But if you love pickles and whiskey, this is your dream shot. Story goes this all started in Philadelphia when a shot of Irish whiskey was served in a bar, immediately followed by a shot of pickle juice from the jar to help temper the heat of the alcohol. Now so popular you can buy ready-made pickle juice in bottles to add to cocktails (especially good in a Bloody Mary) but it's just as easy to make your own. Scale up this recipe if you want to actually pickle something in the juice, but this is enough to make pickle juice for around 10 pickleback shots.

300ml water
200ml cider vinegar
140g demerara sugar
Generous pinch of salt flakes
Pinch of herbs and spices (bay leaf, peppercorns, coriander seeds, fennel seeds, cardamom pods)
Irish whiskey

Put the water in a pan and add the vinegar and sugar. Heat gently and stir to dissolve the sugar, then add the salt and flavourings. Turn the heat off and leave to cool. When cool, strain the liquid into a clean jar or bottle.

To make a pickleback, pour one shot of whiskey into a shot glass and a shot of pickle juice into another. Shoot the whiskey before chasing it with the pickle juice. First-timers be warned, it's a real love it or hate it drink. But you won't know if you don't try.

4

ALCOHOL-FREE COCKTAILS

For days when you're off the booze, these are fun to make, beautiful to look at and delicious to drink. They just don't have a drop of alcohol in them.

STRAWBELLINI

For this, you need a bottle of Seedlip, the non-alcoholic spirit.
Not cheap, but one bottle lasts for ages. Use it as you would
gin – treat it as the base (non-alcoholic) spirit and add mixers
and flavours. This one uses a slug of your homemade
strawberry shrub.

25ml Seedlip Garden
25ml chilled Strawberry & Basil Shrub (see page 57)
Soda water
Fresh strawberry or sprig of fresh basil

Chill your flute or coupe in the freezer for a couple of minutes.
Add the Seedlip and shrub, top up with chilled soda water and
garnish with a slice of strawberry and/or a sprig of fresh basil.

COCO-RITA

I first tried something like this in the brilliant booze-free bar Redemption in London. Like a Margarita but without the hit of tequila, this relies on lots of fresh lime and coconut to help you forget that there's no alcohol in the glass. Makes enough for two coupes or one larger serving in a tumbler.

Wedges of lime
Crushed sea salt flakes
150ml coconut water
20ml fresh lime juice
10ml sugar syrup

Salt the rim of your glass (or half the rim if you prefer) by rubbing a wedge of lime around the top and then dipping it into crushed salt flakes. Put a handful of ice into a cocktail shaker and pour in the coconut water, lime juice and sugar syrup. Give it all a good shake and strain into the glass(es). Garnish with a wedge of lime.

STRAWBERRY & THYME SPRITZ

———

Definitely worth the less-than-five-minute hassle it takes to make. This makes enough for two servings.

5 fresh strawberries
15ml Earl Grey tea syrup (see page 63, or use simple sugar syrup instead)
20ml fresh lemon juice
3 sprigs of fresh thyme
Soda water

Put the strawberries into a cocktail shaker with the syrup (if using), the lemon juice and the leaves from one of the thyme sprigs and muddle gently. Add a handful of ice and shake. Strain into two small ice-filled tumblers or pour half and save the other half in the shaker in the fridge for another one later. Be warned: it's a slow pourer because there's so much strawberry flesh so don't try and strain it through a sieve. Just rely on the strainer on the top of the cocktail shaker – or if using a jam jar, pour slowly with the lid in place to stop any lumps getting into the glass. Top up with soda water and garnish with a sprig of fresh thyme.

LAVENDER LEMONADE

Quick to make and refreshing to drink, the lavender flavour gives it a real summery edge. Close your eyes and you could be in Provence. Kind of.

30ml lavender syrup (see page 64)
30ml fresh lemon juice
Soda water
Sprig of fresh lavender or twist of lemon peel

Put a handful of ice into a tumbler. Add the lavender syrup and lemon juice and stir gently. Top up with soda water and add a sprig of fresh lavender if you have one. Otherwise a twist of lemon peel does the trick.

SAGE & BLUEBERRY SMASH

You can make this with any seasonal soft fruit and herb combination you like – raspberry and mint, blackberries and thyme, blood orange and rosemary – but I especially love the subtle flavours of this particular combination.

10 fresh blueberries, plus a few to garnish
4–5 fresh sage leaves, plus a couple to garnish
30ml fresh lemon juice
5ml (1 tsp) honey (or a dash of sugar syrup
if you don't like honey)
Soda water

Put the blueberries and sage leaves into a cocktail shaker, add the lemon juice and honey and muddle gently. Add a handful of ice and shake. Strain into a small ice-filled tumbler (you might have to shift the sage leaves to the side if it doesn't strain easily) and top up with soda water. Garnish with a few blueberries and a couple of sage leaves.

LAST ORDERS

WHEN I FIRST STARTED THINKING ABOUT THIS BOOK, I knew I wanted to write a simple cocktail guide that would help me make more cocktails – because as much as I loved them, I hardly ever made them at home. What's more, there is real joy in making someone a drink they're not expecting, something a little more glamorous than a glass of white. Yes, it creates a bit more mess and takes a few moments longer than opening a bottle, but if you're in good company and they love what you've made for them, it's properly, life-affirmingly wonderful.

Now, go and break the ice.

ACKNOWLEDGEMENTS

SO MANY PEOPLE HAVE HELPED ME WITH THIS BOOK, not least my brilliant friends and family (luckily, they all have rubber arms when asked if they'd like a drink). Enormous thanks to Craig Harper and Sam Carter, both of whom know far more than I do about cocktails and helped me understand what makes a good one. Also to Dawn Davis, Lucy Shaw, Jim Mills, Boris Iván and Ian Wisniewski for their generous insights and to Joe Wadsack for taking me to the Pink Chihuahua all those years ago and lighting my tequila fire. Thanks to my friend and fellow wino Victoria Moore for her support, always (and her thunderous gin & tonics). Thank you to my very special agent Heather Holden-Brown and her team; to Maggie Ramsay and to Duncan Proudfoot, Jess Gulliver and Amanda Keats at Robinson for making this all happen. Enormous thanks as well to designer Andrew Barron for the wonderful illustrations. Next round is on me. Finally, thank you Ross for pretty much everything, really.

FURTHER REFERENCE

Follow my blog for weekly drinks recommendations:
www.knackeredmotherswineclub.com
Instagram: @knackeredmother
Facebook: knackeredmotherswineclub
Twitter: @knackeredmutha

BOOKS

The Fine Art of Mixing Drinks David A. Embury (Faber, 1953)
How to Drink Victoria Moore (Granta, 2009)
Modern British Food Sybil Kapoor (Penguin, 1996)
Regarding Cocktails Sasha Petraske (Phaidon, 2016)
Esquire's Handbook for Hosts (Frederick Muller Ltd, 1954)

INDEX

TASTING NOTES

_____
_____
_____
_____
_____
_____
_____
_____
_____
_____
_____
_____
_____
_____
_____
_____
_____
_____
_____
_____
_____

HOMEMADE COCKTAILS **150**